Study Smarts

How to Learn More in Less Time

Study Smarts

How to Learn More in Less Time

Judi Kesselman-Turkel and Franklynn Peterson

Contemporary Books, Inc.
Chicago

Library of Congress Cataloging-in-Publication Data

Kesselman-Turkel, Judi.
  Study smarts.

  Bibliography: p.
  1. Study, Method of.   I. Peterson, Franklynn.
II. Title.
LB1049.K47   371.3'028'12   81-66084
ISBN 0-8092-5852-8 (pbk.)   AACR2

Published by Contemporary Books, Inc.
Two Prudential Plaza, Chicago, Illinois 60601-6790
(312) 540-4500
Manufactured in the United States of America
International Standard Book Number: 0-8092-5852-8

Published simultaneously in Canada by Fitzhenry & Whiteside
195 Allstate Parkway, Markham, Ontario L3R 4T8
Canada

For Jeff, starting college . . .

CONTENTS

PART II: REMEMBERING TIPS

DON'T READ THIS

We assume that you've picked up this book because you'd like some help. You're not getting the grades you think you should, or you're spending too much time working for those grades. Or maybe both.

If so, you came to the right place. Effective studying is the one thing guaranteed to get you higher grades. You can read all the assigned material, do all the assigned homework, write papers like mad—but if you don't know how to learn what you're supposed to and digest it enough to spew it back on the exam, you can work your butt off and still fail.

If you're like most people, you think of studying as reviewing, and that's what you expect a book on studying to help you with. But you can't review what you don't know in the first place. Studying has two parts: *learning* and *remembering*.

There's been a lot of recent scientific research into studying. For example, one researcher proved that it's not how much *time* you study that counts, but how *well*. In his investigation, students who studied more than 35 hours a week came out with poorer grades than those who studied less than 30.

Scientists now understand how people learn and how they remember, and we've collected their findings. In most cases, we won't cite evidence or describe experiments. Our goal is to give you quick and simple guidelines for getting more out of studying, so you can start to use some of them while you still want to try. If you'd like to read all the hows and whys, consult the Appendix for books that go into greater detail.

Begin this book by skimming through, skipping what you think you're good at and concentrating on a hint here and a tip there. Any one guideline is sure to help you. But we hope that once you've tried a few and found that they work, you'll go back and read from start to finish. Followed from beginning to end, the book is guaranteed to make your final exam reviewing short, efficient, and productive.

PART I:

LEARNING TIPS

LEARNING TIP 1

Beg, Borrow, or Make a Course Outline

Before an A student cracks a book or walks into a classroom, he's usually got a pretty good idea of what the course is about. He's reread the description in the catalog, asked what the professor's like, tried to find out what's going to be expected of him.

That's not cheating. It's an important way of getting a fix on the whole before you're so immersed that all you can see each week is one tiny part. If you take some time right at the beginning to get a perspective, a sharp focus on what's coming, you'll be able to put all your notes into perspective again for the final exam.

The best device for getting—and keeping—this perspective is a course outline. In some schools, these outlines are for sale by the Student Union or some other enterprising group. Some professors give them out the first day of class. If you can't get one from either source, make your own before the first class from the units and chapters in your textbook. It may not be entirely accurate, or in the correct sequence, but it will give you an overview of what you're going to learn this semester.

Why not just *read* the table of contents, since in many cases you'll be copying it? For two reasons.

(1) In order to write, your mind has to think, so it can eliminate such headings as "summary," "problems," and "projects." It will also begin to decode the strange words—and there'll be lots of them. What seems like a foreign language when you're just reading, suddenly will begin to make a little sense when you write it all down.

(2) In writing, you're going to learn, quickly and easily,

the sound and maybe even the spelling of some terms that are fundamental to the course. Your first day in the lecture hall will be less like walking into a foreign country.

For English and Social Studies, you may have many assigned texts. In cases where that's true, list each book's title and topic. Then be a detective. Find the threads that tie the readings together. Are half on socialism and the other half on communism? That in itself tells you a lot about the focus of the course.

A second way to put the course in perspective is to pinpoint its demands. Again, don't just think about this. Make a list—do it on the course outline—of which of the following are expected of you: quizzes, long tests, homework, papers. Put down as many details about them as you know; how many of each kind, when due, length, type (essay tests or short answers, research papers or personal essays), and any other information that will help you to prepare better for them.

Pinpoint the course demands in another way, too. List the kinds of information you'll be expected to know at the end: facts, formulas, dates, details—or is this an ideas course in which you'll be tested on whether you've formed conclusions or gotten the big picture? (Most social studies courses are examples of the last.)

If a friend offers to show you her notes, tests, or papers from the same class, use them now to get a focus on the course. But don't buy them, or even keep using them for free, even if you've got the same teacher. They're hot potatoes. If held too long, they'll burn you badly. Borrowing from someone else's paper, even partially, is treated like a crime if you're caught. And depending on someone else's notes will actually lower your grade. You'll see why in Learning Tip 9.

LEARNING TIP 2

Figure Out What the Goal Is

You probably haven't thought much about *why*. You're in school, so you take courses. You're in courses, so you go to classes, do some reading, and prepare some assignments. Sometimes you probably feel like you're dreaming it's all happening.

The problem is, people rarely remember their dreams. In order to remember, you've got to force your experiences to make a dent on your brain. (Research scientists can tell you just where the dents occur. They can even show you pictures of the dents.)

To make the dents, you need motivation. To help you find some motives, think about *why*. Here are some answers to think about, too.

Why are you supposed to read the assigned book? If it's a fact book, you're reading for information. If it's a book about someone's ideas, it's for understanding. If it's fiction, you're reading for fun—but also critically, to see how it was put together and why the author did it that way. If you're reading a number of books on one topic, it may be to create your own attitude toward the topic, by picking and choosing from the bunch.

Why go to class in addition to doing the reading? To get help with the facts or ideas you're reading about. Otherwise, you could get an independent education and wouldn't need college at all. (If you're one of the rare people who doesn't need much help, investigate your school's Independent Study offerings.)

The point of a professor's lectures is either: (1) to highlight the important points in the course (which may not all be in the book); (2) to explain the facts and ideas that are pres-

ented in the book—or maybe to explain just the difficult
ones; or (3) to challenge what you're reading, so that you'll
think more about it and—perhaps—come up with your own
ideas. If the lecturer is doing any one of these things, it pays
to go to class.

Why take basic courses? (They're often boring and sometimes sloppily taught.) To give you the background information, the vocabulary, the basic formulas, and the working
methods you'll need if you ever do any further investigation
in this particular area of knowledge—or in related areas, as
in the case of taking calculus to prepare for science or
economics courses.

What's the point of learning a foreign language? Are you
planning to speak it some day, or just to read it in your
work? (For example, many important scientific papers are
written in German.) Knowing the point of taking the course
will help you decide whether to learn every word precisely or
to aim for free translation, and whether to spend more time
on speaking or on writing. (It may also point you to the
instructor whose teaching goals are closest to your learning
goals.) If you don't have any point in learning the language,
maybe you ought to consider dropping it for now. Few
schools require a foreign language for graduation anymore,
and Mama's insistence that every educated person needs a
second language won't motivate anyone but Mama through
the grueling memory work that language courses entail.

LEARNING TIP 3

Learn the Special Vocabulary

Every course has its special vocabulary. You'll study faster if you isolate those words and learn what they mean. Sometimes a word you know well suddenly takes on a specific meaning, and for that course all other meanings are wrong. Watch for these words especially; they're tricky. (For example, *specific* means one thing in our sentence above, but in *specific gravity* it means something else.)

Keep 3 × 5 cards close at hand when you listen, read, and review. Each time the book or your professor defines a term, write the term on one side of the card and its definition on the other. This has two advantages: (1) writing makes more of a dent in your memory than just reciting; (2) you've started a permanent cram file for tests.

Sometimes you'll find a new term that isn't defined by the teacher or the book. It's probably one that was defined in a previous course most of the class had. Before you settle for the dictionary definition, ask a professor. It may turn out to be (1) something he'd better teach the entire class, in which case he'll be grateful, or (2) a clue to a big gap in *your* preparatory learning—maybe something you missed in twelfth grade because you were home with the flu.

There's more to vocabulary than words. Math, science, even social science courses rely on basic symbols. Make sure that they, too, go on your vocabulary cards if they're new to you. Formulas are basic vocabulary in some courses.

Do you know how to read graphs, tables, charts, diagrams, drawings, and photos? If you've never learned, see if your school study center gives a short course you can enroll in. It's tempting to skip over these illustrations, but that's like skipping the book introduction. Like the introduction, illustrations are put there to help *you,* not the author. If you stop and figure out what they mean, you're guaranteed to remember what they tell you. (We'll have more to say about why these *visuals* are such memory imprinters in Remembering Tip 8.)

What do you do if a book seems like it's *all* written in some special vocabulary? (Many times, we've felt as if we were over our heads in long sentences that made little sense.) Usually, it's not your fault but the fault of bad writing. Some authors, especially in education and social sciences, spew out a large amount of jargon. Sometimes you can make sense of it if you read it aloud. Sometimes it's worthwhile to search for a more clearly written book on the same topic, and to read the appropriate part of that one first. Your instructor may be able to point you in the right direction. If not, ask for help from the department chair or whomever chooses books for similar courses.

Especially if you're not interested in the subject, try to find an easier book that explains it. You'll do much better on exams if you understand a simplified idea completely than if you only partially understand a complicated one.

LEARNING TIP 4

Skim Book Prefaces, Intros, and Such

The reason we headed our introduction "Don't Read This" was to try to get you to at least skim it. Like most authors, we put a lot of important information into those few paragraphs.

(1) We told you why this book that's supposed to be about studying has hints for *learning* and *remembering* and seems to have none for *studying*. Without understanding why we chose those main topics, you're going to have trouble figuring out the point of the book.

(2) We told you that we're presenting only facts for which we've found scientific evidence—but that you won't find the evidence for most of the facts here. Unless you read that, you're going to think this is a very top-of-the-head book and wonder about how valuable it really is.

(3) We suggested how to use the book for best results.

You probably got used to skipping intros after trying a few in grade school. There, the textbook intros were written for teachers, not students. And the intros to novels were often dull facts about the author's life or philosophy. Skipping the introduction didn't hurt your enjoyment of the story one bit.

But for college textbooks, the intros are meant to help you. They may explain the author's point of view, show the organization, define special terms and symbols, and offer hints for best use of the book. In short, they may cut down on your reading and study time.

Introductions are often boring, so don't read every word. But do skim to see what's in them.

LEARNING TIP 5

Cut Your Reading Time in Half

At the hub of most courses is the textbook or the set of required readings. Few teachers cover everything that's in the books in class, but most expect you to remember all their contents on tests. Interest helps your mind remember, but it's hard to work up enthusiasm when you've got twenty pounds of difficult pages to get through in four months.

Simply reading a chapter from start to finish doesn't work on most textbooks, mostly because part of your mind is wishing you were finished. One researcher found that the average person forgets half the ideas he reads within a few minutes. To make any impression that your mind can remember, you need to give the ideas or facts complete attention. If you find yourself backtracking words, phrases, or even paragraphs, you're *nonreading*, not reading. It's a waste of your time.

Several systems have been devised that keep your reading in sharp focus, with hard-to-forget acronyms like SQ3R, OK4R, PANORAMA, REAP, PQRST, and even OARWET. They've been proven to work, too, if you stick with any one of them. Here's our own modification of Dr. Walter Pauk's OK4R system:

O. *Overview:* Read the title, the introductory and summarizing paragraphs, and all the headings. Read everything in italics and bold type, and all bulleted (●) sections, itemizations, pictures, and tables: in other words, everything that stands out from the ordinary text. You'll end up with a very good idea of the topics in your homework selection.

K. *Key ideas:* Now *skim* the text for the key ideas. (We'd like to call this part *S* because skimming is what's important. But OK4R, being catchier, is easier to remember than OS4R.)

R1. *Read* your assignment from beginning to end. *Do it quickly.* You'll be able to, because you already know where the author is going and what he's trying to prove. (If you slow up, you're going to start thinking about other things and you'll start forgetting more than you remember.)

R2. *Rite:* Put aside the text and *write,* in a few key words or sentences, the major points of what you've read. Since most forgetting takes place right after initial learning, and writing is twice as effective a memory jog as just thinking, *one minute* spent right away writing down what you read actually *doubles* the amount that you'll fix in your brain. (Don't try to shortcut by copying the author's summary. It's wasted effort. You won't learn a thing unless you filter the information through your brain.)

R3. *Relate:* To really keep the material in your mind forever, connect it in with what you already know. The best way is to find some personal significance or strong image for what you've read. You'll find other ways scattered through the Remembering Tips.

R4. *Review:* This step doesn't take place right away. It should be done for the next short quiz, and then again for later tests throughout the term. Several reviews will make that knowledge indelibly yours. (See Remembering Tip 6.)

If you get a pen and some paper, we'll prove to you that the system works. Read the title of this section: *Cut Your Reading Time in Half.* Now read OK4R: Overview, Key ideas, Read, Rite, Relate, Review. We've helped you do the OK part; now *reread* the whole section quickly to here. Once that's done, *rite* what we said—just a few key words.

We wrote down: to remember textbook material: (1) interest, (2) systems: OK4R preferred. Overview (general idea), Key ideas (skim), R1 Read (fast), R2 Rite (1 minute), R3 Relate (connect in mind), R4 Review (later).

Let's do the R3 together, the part about making connections in your mind. In our minds, this system is similar to the way you'd open a birthday gift. First you try to guess the contents from the box's size and shape (overview). Then you jiggle it for a key to what's inside (key words). You open it and *read* the label. It's an electric finger-warmer. You w*rite* a thank-you note saying how handy it'll be at the next football game (relate). Then you put it away—and forget you own it unless you remember it from time to time (review).

We chose to relate OK4R to a birthday gift image. You could have selected the image of doing a picture puzzle, visiting a strange resort, or anything else that seems similar to the procedure to *you*. Relating is fun once you get the hang of it—and it's the best memorizing device known.

If you rebel against systems and aren't willing to try OK4R, here's a four-step procedure to try. This one also works for novels and for nontextbook nonfiction like articles, essays, and source materials.

(1) *Skim.* Read titles and skim pages, reading whatever catches your eye. If you find any summaries, read them, but only after you've skimmed all the pages.

(2) *Read.* Read the whole selection quickly, penciling check marks next to important parts and parts that you can't understand.

(3) *Probe.* Go back and reread the parts you've checked until you understand them thoroughly. Now that you've read the whole section, some of those parts will make sense without further effort.

(4) *Write.* Sum up the main idea, significant details, and conclusions, *in your own words,* either in outline form or in sentences or in patterns (see Learning Tip 9), whichever form makes the most sense.

Or try your own system. Anything is more effective than just trudging through from start to finish—and faster, too, we guarantee.

Some reading systems suggest that you figure out questions to ask yourself while you read. But if you haven't got any background on a topic, finding questions takes more time than it's worth. Some systems advise you to read the first sentence of every paragraph before you read through the entire selection. But few authors consciously remember to put a paragraph's topic in the first sentence. Sometimes it's there; often it isn't. Skimming the entire passage quickly is generally just as effective.

The point of skimming should be to work up some interest in reading what the author has to say. If an interesting sentence here and there catches your eye, you've accomplished the purpose.

LEARNING TIP 6
Beware the Over-Underlined Textbook

Of course, if the book doesn't belong to you, you won't be underlining at all. But if you underline, do it sparingly. The best underlining is not going to help you remember as much as the worst note-taking. Your goal should be to be able to explain what's in a chapter, in the most stripped-down terms.

Over-underlining is usually the result of following some teacher's favorite textbook-learning system. You've been told, "As you read, underline all the key words and phrases, the definitions, the quotable points, and the examples." Once you've done all that, there isn't much left un-underlined.

The first tip for combating that is: *never* underline at all until you've first skimmed the entire selection, and try to keep it to *one* underline per paragraph. One researcher found that 30 percent of passages you mark on a first reading aren't important at all. If you must underline the first time through, do it in pencil.

The second tip is: *rarely* underline fiction or outside readings. You'll find yourself concentrating on minutiae when it's the big picture you really want. Instead, use the front inside cover of your book to note significant pages and—briefly—why; on the page put a check in the margin at the important item. (If it's a borrowed book, you can staple a piece of paper onto the title page.) For example, our copy of *Walden's* inside cover looks like this:

12—what's necessary
14—who book is for
19—clothing conventions
28—civilized vs savage
36—building his house

53-4—costs
61—auctions
64—against reg. houses (219 too)
79—astronomy
90—reading classics
106-7—brilliant satire (116)
112—contradiction (122)
139—sarcasm: intoll. of humans (145)
157+—beauty of pond (165-6, 256)
191—hunting, sport vs killing
193—vegetarian
223—scientific conclusion (258)
253—transcendentalism (259, 273)
280—Emersonian (283, 285)
293—humility
?—42, 69, 70, 73, 79, 80, 131, 143
good quotes—29, 33, 63, 82, 100, 174, 288

On some page margins we've put our own thoughts and conclusions. We've asked specific questions in a few places. We've circled words we didn't understand, hoping to look them up. (Later, we figured most of them out fairly well from the context.)

It's a good idea to read with a pencil. It helps you stay awake and alert. But we don't advocate systems that include four colors of ink and six kinds of marks, mainly because they're not your system but someone else's. It's been scientifically proven that any system *you* devise or adapt is better than anyone else's system that you try to copy whole hog. That's partly because thoughts that are focused on trying to remember a system won't be focused on trying to remember what you read.

If you're buying second-hand books, *never* buy one that's been underlined in pen, and if the underlining is in pencil, erase it before you start reading. Otherwise, you'll tend to rely on the other person's underlining—and you'll never know whether the hand that held the pen got an A or an F in the course.

LEARNING TIP 7

Be Class-Smart: Go Early, Stay Late

The first five minutes of class are the next-to-most important. Teachers rarely jump into a subject without first either *reviewing* enough to put today's words into perspective, or *previewing,* summarizing the day's thoughts to come. Some lecturers do both. Grab that opportunity for your own review, or to prepare a tentative outline for the day's lecture. If you jot down the main ideas that are crammed into those first five minutes, they'll be among your most valuable notes.

The *last* five minutes are the most important. The organized teacher uses that time to sum up the main ideas she just covered. Review along with her, and fill in the notes you missed.

Often a teacher gets sidetracked and runs out of time. She may jam up to a half hour's content into the last five or ten minutes of the lecture. She may say it quickly and in little more than outline form—but she probably expects you to know it all for the next test. So work like crazy to get down that packed few minutes' worth. Stay after class, if you need to, to finish getting it down. It'll be hard, because people who are less savvy than you will be packing their gear away and putting on their coats, but it usually pays off better than an extra hour of studying.

Listening in class is like riding a bike. Once you learn how, it's easy—but only if you stay sharp. If you don't keep awake on your bike, you may hit a pothole or run into a turning car.

Most lecturers talk about ten times as slowly as students take notes. That's nine minutes of possible drifting time for every minute of alertness, and once you drift you may miss the next important turn. Especially treacherous are the teachers who speak in monotone or unusual accents, or who mumble or race. The best defense is to sit up front so that you're forced to pay more attention. With foreign accents, decipher the problem sounds at the beginning of the course so that if Prof says, "The georagy of the Apparachians," you can train your ear to translate: "The geology of the Appalachians."

If you know you're not a good listener, you can train your ears by playing records and forcing yourself to memorize the words of songs with as few playings as possible, or by summing up the main points of TV news shows. But the best booster of listening power is the act of taking notes.

LEARNING TIP 8

Catch the Lecturer's Clues

As the lecturer speaks, your notes have to convert his words into the following:

(1) Title: main idea, topic, thesis, rule, or principle. (It's possible for there to be several titles in one lecture, or one title spanning several consecutive lectures.)

(2) Subordinate topics: the pieces that fit together to form the main idea.

(3) Supports: the definitions, explanations, examples, and proofs of all the topic's pieces.

If the lecturer follows a strict outline, your job is easy. The more he tends to ramble, the tougher it is to take notes. But his words and his style will help you, if you know what to look for.

The first clue is his overall approach. Does he stick to the textbook, following it along chapter by chapter and page by page? If so, you can outline or map what he'll cover *before* you go to class, and just fill in while you listen. Does he just zero in on the hard parts? If so, a preview reading of the chapter is vital. Does he focus on just the important facts or ideas? If so, skim the chapter before class and then again afterward. Do his lectures supplement the book, providing unrelated information you won't find there? Then you've got to take fuller notes, but your textbook reading can often be done at your leisure.

Time is an important clue, too. The more time devoted to an idea, the more important the lecturer usually considers it. Does she give lots of examples? Does she take the time to write it on the board? Does she bring in a film or prepared slides for overhead projection? Does she repeat one thought several times, either in the same words or in different ones?

Then you can practically bet that the fact or idea she's taking more time with will show up on an exam.

Another clue to organizing your notetaking is in the material itself. Learn to recognize the three basic types of organization: *chronological* (in time sequence), *spacial* (what's next to what; for example, organizing the planets in order of closeness to the sun), and *logical*. The last kind of organization is the trickiest, and is used in most college subjects. To help you, we've included a chart from our textbook *Good Writing*.

Other clues are words that say, "I'm summarizing." *Therefore* and *in essence* are words like that. An important definition may follow the words "it means . . ." On the other hand, you may be getting just a rambling explanation, so keep alert.

When you take notes on your reading, you can put ideas into your own words. But when you take lecture notes, be sure to copy the lecturer's pet words and phrases. She'll use—and expect you to use—those words on your exams.

HOW MOST IDEAS ARE ORGANIZED LOGICALLY*

GROUP 1. In time sequence:
- in the sequence in which it was seen or done
- in the sequence in which it should be seen or done
- from cause to effect

GROUP 2. From general to specific:
- general topic to subtopics
- theoretical to practical
- generalization to examples

GROUP 3. From least to most:
- easiest to hardest
- smallest to largest
- worst to best
- weakest to strongest
- least important to most important
- least complicated to most complicated
- least effective to most effective
- least controversial to most controversial

GROUP 4. From most to least:
- most known to least known
- most factual to least factual (fact to opinion)

GROUP 5. Giving both sides (grouped or interspersed):
- pros and cons
- similarities and differences (compare and contrast)
- assets and liabilities
- hard and easy
- bad and good
- effective and ineffective
- weak and strong
- complicated and uncomplicated
- controversial and uncontroversial

*Reprinted from *Good Writing* by Judi Kesselman-Turkel and Frank-lynn Peterson (Franklin Watts, 1981).

LEARNING TIP 9

Learn by Taking Organized Notes

This tip doesn't suggest that you should take notes in order to learn. It actually promises that you will learn just by taking notes. A recent study proved that people who took lecture notes did much better on a test given weeks later—even without reviewing their notes—than people who didn't take any notes.

Why did it work? Because the no-notes group just sat and let it all flow past them, while the note-takers had to think about what was being said so that they could select the items they wanted to write down.

So even if you don't know how to take notes, plunge in and begin taking some. It's like skating—you'll get better at it with practice.

Your notes will sink in best if they're organized. Most of the time, as we pointed out in Learning Tip 8, you should include the main topic, the subordinate topics (ideas, general statements, and conclusions), and all the details (definitions, examples, and explanations) that support them. If you're still not sure how to recognize a topic from a detail, or how to outline or summarize, get help in your school study center. You can't remember anything well until you've learned how to organize and reduce words to their essentials. (Several publishers market *course outline* books. Most are good examples of how to outline.)

Quite a bit of research has been done on note-taking, and until recently one system was considered the best for everyone. We'll describe it first.

Use 8½ × 11-inch looseleaf paper and write on *just one side*. (This may seem wasteful, but it's one time when economizing is secondary.) Head each page with a main topic. Then take the time to rule your page as follows:

(1) If the course is one in which lecture and text are closely related, use the 2-3-3-2 technique. Make columns of two inches down the left-hand side for memory clues, three inches in the middle for lecture notes, and three inches on the right side for textbook notes. Leave a two-inch space across the bottom for your own observations and conclusions.

(2) If it's a course where the lectures and the reading are not closely related, use separate pages for class notes and reading notes, following the 2-5-1 technique: two inches at left for clues, five in the middle for notes, and an inch at the right for your own observations. (After a while you won't need to draw actual lines.)

In the center section or sections belong your regular notes, taken in the form you've evolved during your years of schooling. The clue column is the key to higher grades. As soon as possible after you've written your notes, take the time to read them over—don't study them, just read them. Check now, while it's still all fresh, to see whether you've left out anything important or put down anything incorrectly, and make your changes. Then, in that left-hand column, set down clue words to the topics in your notes.

These clue words should not repeat information, but should label or pinpoint whatever you'll need to remember. They're the kind of clues you would put on crib sheets. For example, to remember the information contained so far in this section on note-taking, you need just the following clues:

organize: main topic, subordinates, details
paper: 8½ × 11 looseleaf, 1 side
2-3-3-2
2-5-1
l-h col. = clue words

As you can see, they're fast reminders. They're what you'll use later on in sharpening your long-term memory.

The beauty of the clue-word note-taking method is that it provides a painless way to do the one thing proved most conducive to remembering what you learn: actively thinking about your notes and making logical sense of them. If, instead of having to think up clues, you just keep going over your recorded notes, you'll not only get bored but you'll be trying to remember in the least effective way.

Notice that we suggest notes for both lectures and reading. If it sounds like too much work, make a mental image of all those people mentioned in the first paragraph of this section who, just by taking notes, got much higher test scores.

Notes on a *book* should be translated into your own words. It'll help you understand better and remember longer. In most cases, however, take down a *lecturer's* precise terminology. For example, if Prof says, "There are three types of decision problems: queues, games, and linear programming," don't write:

> deciding: queues
> games
> line programs

or you won't recognize the cue words "decision problems" or "linear programming" when they appear on the test. Instead write:

> decision problems: 3 types
> queues
> games
> linear programming

Don't attempt frantically to get down the entire lecture. It's been shown that people who take too many notes do poorly on tests. For most lectures, aim for getting down about 20 percent of what's said. Concentrate on what you don't already know. If the lecturer is a speed demon, or if you get lost, or if you're the kind who really can't listen and write at the same time, jot down just a few clue words and leave lots of blank space. At the end of class, fill it in. You'll be able to remember most of it. (Don't wait much longer than that, or you won't recall a thing.)

There's a new kind of note-taking that works well for experienced notetakers who can pick out words easily, and for people who enjoy mathematical games. It's called *mapping* or *patterning*. It works best when you're dealing with ideas, as in social science courses, or with things that you must divide into smaller and smaller parts. For example, the parts of a cell, the members of the animal kingdom, and an analysis of Freud's theories all lend themselves to this kind of note-taking. It works like this:

Within a circle, square, star, or any other pattern centered on a page, you print the overall topic of the lecture or book selection. Then you draw lines out from the topic to rest the main ideas on. (Printing is an important part of this system, so don't scrawl in longhand.) Supporting ideas branch off from the major ideas. They include definitions, examples, and such. Here's our pattern of the OK4R reading method outlined in Learning Tip 5.

A variation of patterning, the *pyramid,* works well in showing a main topic that includes a number of lesser ideas. (The left side of our pyramid, shown here, is more free-form than the right side.)

You can make up other types of maps, too. For example, chronological information fits best on a time-line pattern. Comparative information is most clearly shown on a chart. Parts of a whole can be drawn on pie graphs. Once you have the hang of patterning, you'll find you can write less and remember more.

Patterning has many advantages over traditional outline-form note-taking:

(1) You have to think and organize before you write. You can't just passively copy a lecture. That in itself helps you remember twice as much as before.

A Pattern for Remembering OK4R

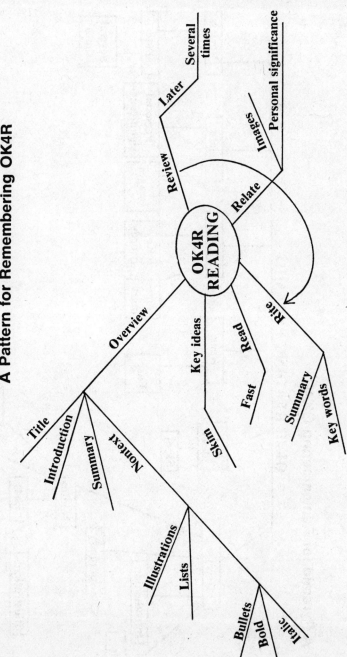

A Pyramid for Remembering OK4R

OK4R READING PYRAMID

- **Overview**
  - Title
  - Introduction
  - Summary
  - **Nontext**
    - Illustrations
    - Bullets
    - Lists
    - Bold
    - Italic
- **Key ideas**
  - Skim
- **Read**
  - Fast
- **Rite**
  - Summary
  - Key words
- **Relate**
  - Images
  - Personal significance
- **Review**
  - Later
    - Several times

(2) You can see the topic at a glance.

(3) The links between ideas are shown clearly. (Notice that in our pattern we're able to add an arrow that shows we review what we wrote during the Rite stage.) Association is a powerful prod to your memory.

(4) Because patterning is so graphic, you remember longer.

(5) No two patterns look alike. That too helps memory.

(6) You can add new information easily where it belongs, even if the Prof skips around.

(7) You can use your creativity in forming the patterns. It helps make note-taking a challenge instead of a drag.

Because you'll remember more after you've done your own thinking, organizing, and note-taking, you can see why someone else's notes can hurt more than help. Worst of all, trusting someone else's notes means you have to trust someone else for accuracy.

Similarly, once you get actively involved in thinking about the information, you'll decide for yourself that bringing a tape recorder to class is the worst self-defeater ever suggested. Users think it frees them to pay total attention to what's going on, but studies have proven that it makes you *less* attentive, not more. In addition, once you have a tape, you have to listen to it a second, third, and fourth time to really remember much of what's on it. You'll find it more effective to take notes on the tape and study them—which you could have done more easily in class in the first place.

The same students who underline too much in their textbooks tend to take too many notes. In math and science lectures, especially, it's sometimes best to take down just the principles, definitions, formulas, and rules, and perhaps one illustration for each.

In science laboratory classes, on the other hand, you must write down every detail, even the ones you think you'll remember. Each department has its own rules for how lab reports are to be presented, but one common rule is that you record *all* observations and calculations. Most students write their lab reports at home, but here's a tip: check to see if you've got plausible results *before* you put away your equipment. If your answer's way off base, you may be able to find the reason right there and then.

LEARNING TIP 10

Devise a Lecture Shorthand

If you don't have your own lecture shorthand, start to make up one. Don't try a large number of new abbreviations and symbols at once, or you'll end up with a set of hieroglyphics you won't be able to read. Add one or two new shortcuts a week, and note-taking is guaranteed to become less of a chore.

Speedwriting books have lots of ideas you can borrow quickly. For example, they suggest using a "g" for "ing":

Developg countries are growg stronger.

Another adaptable idea is to eliminate vowels:

Dvlpg cntries are growg strngr.

The trick here is to eliminate only the vowels that can disappear without the word being mistaken for others in context. For example, *cntrs* could be *centers* as well as *countries,* so we keep the *ie* clue. Usually, the longer the word the more easily it can be recognized without any of its vowels; the shorter the word, the easier it'll be to read back if you leave the vowels in (*growg* vs. *grwg*).

You can borrow symbols you know from other subjects: < for *is less than,* ∿ for *is similar to* or just *similar,* = for *is the same as.*

The purpose of your symbols and abbreviations is to make note-taking easier *without giving up easy readability.* If it takes you more time to think of the symbol than to write out the word, forget the symbol. If you can't remember the symbol when you read back your notes, discard the symbol. The final product *must* be easy to read.

For the same reason, it's important that *you* make up the system. Trying to learn someone else's complete system is like taking a foreign language course. The best systems are the ones that you build up slowly over the years.

There are also shorthand ways to clue what's important in your notes: underlines, stars, checks, and other marks. Clue the points the Prof says she'll come back to later. Mark the items she says are common mistakes.

If the lecturer refers to a document—a poem, an article, or a long passage in your book—keep both together in front of you during the lecture. Key each note to the part of the document it refers to by using a number or letter—the same one on both notes and document.

If you're pressed for time in your note-taking, skip copying what's on the board unless your lecturer is eraser-happy. You can usually get boardwork copied during lulls or at the end of class. If your teacher *is* a racer who erases, talk to her about your difficulties.

LEARNING TIP 11

Get It Right the First Time

Have you ever tried to learn a new way of brushing your teeth? Studies show that it's a two-stage procedure—trying to forget the old way as well as learning the new way. Every once in a while, when you aren't thinking hard about brushing, that old devil pattern's going to creep back in.

All learning is like that. It's a lot quicker, easier, and more foolproof to learn something right the first time than to correct something you've learned wrong. And despite your relearning, the wrong answer may be the only one you remember at test-taking time. It's worthwhile to take extra time to get your facts and understandings right on the first attempt.

Listen carefully and copy correctly. It's been demonstrated, for example, that 20 percent of all computation errors are made because the numbers haven't been copied correctly or legibly, or because the person doing the arithmetic hasn't been careful. When writing columns of numbers or lists of statistics, it's important to get them under one another precisely where they belong.

Whether you're solving a problem or defending a conclusion, write down all your steps. It may seem a shortcut to skip past the part that seems obvious or thoroughly known—but that skipped part often turns out to be the careless link that makes the whole thing wrong.

Don't let a half-understood idea get by you. If something is unclear, pinpoint whether it's the facts or the ideas that you're having trouble with. Then track down someone who ought to know and clear up the trouble-spot. *Don't wait.* In most courses, each new concept builds on the ones before it, and that key link you miss may be the one that makes the rest of the course a snap.

LEARNING TIP 12

Preview for Lectures, Prethink for Discussions and Seminars

Ten minutes of preparation before each hour of class time generally saves up to an hour of review time. How does it work? By turning the class time into a structured review. The only time you can't make it work for you is if your professor completely ignores the textbook and covers material you can't anticipate.

For a lecture class, spend the ten minutes skimming the next chapter—or whatever portion of the text is usually covered in a class period. Jot down, on the blank backside of last session's notes, the topic and main subtopics. Also copy all the unfamiliar terms. You'll achieve three goals.

First, you'll be able to recognize what's important in even a rambling lecture, and will organize your notes more quickly and easily.

Second, knowing the language will help you hear correctly, so that when the lecturer mumbles something about "thermionic emission" you won't write "the mionica mission" and need an hour of study time later on just to figure out what he meant.

Third, the lecturer's points will reinforce what you learned while skimming. While your colleagues are listening to new facts and ideas, you'll be getting your first review. You'll even know which parts are harder and, therefore, must be listened to closely and noted in great detail.

Brief preparation is even more helpful when it comes to discussion classes and seminars. Don't just skim the related reading; think about it. If you've noted in advance what's hard to understand, you can ask intelligent questions about it in class. You can also use class time to test out your conclusions *before* you write them on an exam.

In studying a foreign language, it's worthwhile to *always* keep ahead of the class, doing the entire assignment—reading and homework—in advance. Since learning a foreign language is mostly memory work and ear training, you'll turn the class time into a valuable hour of review. Just listen and silently say along the entire lesson, whether it's the teacher or another student who's reciting.

LEARNING TIP 13

Work Through All Sample Problems

An author inserts a sample problem into a book to show how a particular theory works in actual practice. On a test, you'll be expected to know both the theory and the practice. You've probably discovered that the *fastest* way to do homework is to plug the question's numbers into the sample problem. But it's the *worst* way, because it won't help you learn a thing.

Dr. Herbert Lin, who has taught physics at the Massachusetts Institute of Technology, suggests that you study each sample problem or proof that you come to until you're confident that you understand it. Then close the book and work that problem through from memory. If you get stuck, check it against the book; then wait a while and do it again. "Usually these examples are the only problems for which you have a detailed, worked-out solution against which you can check," he says.

Before you even start on a sample problem, be sure that you understand the concept or law it develops. Then, once you understand the procedure from start to finish, do the homework. You'll reinforce what you've just learned, and test problems should be a cinch.

If you're stuck on either the sample or the homework problem because of its complex numbers, try substituting simple ones and working it through that way first. If you get any wrong, *always* redo them from start to finish. You'll learn infinitely more from redoing these mistake problems than from the ones you've gotten correct in the first place.

A classroom teacher doesn't put problems on the board, or bother to work them through, unless they're either important or tricky. Stay alert—copy the problem and follow its explanation. You can bet that you'll have to answer a question having to do with it or its principle on a test.

LEARNING TIP 14

Skim and Pinpoint in Doing Most Outside Reading

Teachers assign outside reading to fill you in on important gaps not covered by the textbook, or to provide background that adds meaning to what the textbook says. Often, you're expected to write papers that show what you've learned.

For some courses, the readings are listed. You've just got to obtain them—usually from a campus library. To get the most out of them, first figure out why they were assigned. For the information? For a different point of view from that in the textbook? Once you know the point of the reading, read quickly, looking for and delving deeply into just what's new or different to you. (For how to take brief notes on outside reading, see Learning Tip 6.)

Often, you're given a topic on which to write, and you have to find your own sources. The first step should be to narrow the focus of your topic—to make it specific enough so that you won't spend too much time researching. (For help in narrowing topics of papers, we suggest Chapter 7 of the authors' textbook, *Good Writing*, which is listed in the Appendix.) For a term paper of more than 2,000 words, you should spend no more than 30 hours of productive time in the library. For a short paper (1,000 words or less) you should be able to research in 8 or 10 hours at the most. When you're recording your notes, be sure to take down the following: author's name, title, date of publication (so you know how current the thinking is), and call number or other information that will enable you to retrieve the publication again quickly.

Most students start with the library card catalog. That's fine if you don't need current information. But most books take several years to write, publish, and stock in the library. If you need current data or ideas, begin with the reference room. The best timesaver there is the reference librarian. Catch her when she's not busy, and tell her your topic. In a few minutes she'll point you toward the information you need, often saving you several hours of search time.

If you don't know about all the resources available in a halfway decent campus library, skim one of the books we've listed in the Appendix. Learn to read summaries and abstracts of journal articles for information: often you can omit reading the article itself. Price the cost of computer searches and discuss your topic with the computer specialist; for a thesis or other lengthy paper, computer searches are often worth the expense in time saved.

Often, the biggest trap in doing outside reading is forgetting to keep your eye on your narrow subject. We pick up a book or an article that has what we need, skim the volume quickly—as we should—and get trapped when our eyes fall on something interesting but irrelevant. We could be reading on for an hour before we realize that the subject has little to do with the topic of research we've chosen.

The only antidote for infectious interest is to keep making yourself skim-and-pinpoint. If your curiosity threatens to get the better of you, start a card file of readings you'd like to go back to some day when you have the time.

If you're having trouble with your assigned class textbook, either because the author's style is muddy or because the words he chooses are complex, you might want to search for an alternative textbook. The first place to go is to your professor or the department chairperson. Copies of most textbooks are sent to the appropriate college department for consideration for use in class, and many departments keep the copies on hand even when they're not assigned. Be honest about stating your needs, so that you can be steered to the book that's best for you. When you get it, don't skim it as if it were outside reading, but read it carefully and completely, chapter by chapter, along with the appropriate assigned reading in the class book. Keep an open mind while you do. You may find that the textbook is better for some topics—or that, while the information is the same in both, the authors' points of view are different.

LEARNING TIP 15

If You Don't Understand, Get Help Fast

If you don't understand a fact or idea thoroughly once you've read it and it's been explained in class, or once the homework assignment on it has been discussed, look for help immediately. It's particularly crucial not to wait if the course is in math or a science, where each new bit of information is built on the step before it. If any one step is rickety, your entire staircase to understanding will collapse.

One way to get help is to look for alternative reading matter. Often there are several ways an idea can be explained, and one author's explanation may make a lot more sense to you than another's.

If you can find a programmed book on the subject, you're in luck. These books are written for people who are learning independently, and they're meticulously prepared so that information is divided into tiny bits. They help you pinpoint exactly which part of a problem you're stumbling over, and aid you in correcting any misconception before you go any further. Computerized programmed courses are equally helpful. Teaching machines and audiovisual aids may also be available in your subject area. Ask in your school study lab for help in finding these materials.

Many textbooks have companion workbooks that offer additional problems and solutions. If your book has one, it's probably mentioned in the introduction or preface, or on the title page. While workbooks rarely contain explanatory text, doing problems and checking them helps you remember a difficult idea or fact.

But by far the best help is a personal tutor—someone you can look in the eye and ask. And the best kind of tutor has the following qualities: he knows the course content cold, he has good judgment about how to teach it, he understands the special problems that confront beginners or slow learners, and—most important—he's anxious to help.

Studies show that, for most people, having a live tutor on just 25 percent of the course content is as good as having a tutor on 100 percent of it—even if you're having lots of trouble with the subject. It's a good point to keep in mind if you're paying the tutor.

There's another point about tutoring that bears remembering. Research shows that, in many cases, *tutors'* grades go up as much as their tutees' grades. That's because, in trying to explain a difficult concept to someone else, you have to fix it clearly in your own mind. It's the reason why studying with a friend is often so helpful even when your friend knows less than you do about the subject. But if you do get help with your ideas from a friend who's not a tutor in the course, be sure that *she* knows what she's talking about. Independently check out whatever you learn from her. To be safe, study first on your own, so that you have some basis to separate fact from half-truth.

PART II:

REMEMBERING TIPS

REMEMBERING TIP 1

Train Your Brain to Think on Cue

As we said in our introduction, studying has two parts: learning and remembering. *Learning* is pinpointing the facts and ideas and understanding them. *Remembering* is putting them into long-term storage in your head. For high test grades, you need to do both parts. (It also helps to be test-wise, and the authors' companion book, *Test-Taking Strategies,* shows you how.)

Remembering happens in two ways—by rote and by association. Rote memory is when you repeat something over and over again. We'll talk more about it in Remembering Tip 13. Associative memory is when you tie two things together in your mind. It's much more reliable than rote, so it's important to use associative memory as much as you can.

Remember Pavlov's dogs salivating every time they heard a bell ring? That's associative memory. Just as Pavlov modified the dogs' behavior so that they would drool on cue, you can modify your behavior so that your brain thinks and remembers on cue.

But Pavlov's dogs wouldn't have salivated at all unless they had been hungry when they heard the bell ring. You won't begin to remember much unless you *want* to. For best results, like the dogs, you must work up some enthusiasm.

So the first cue is to manufacture some *reason* for wanting to remember what you're studying, even if it's just anticipating questions about it on the final exam. You'll have the least trouble remembering if you're convinced that the thing is worth remembering, but research shows that it pays to find any significance or usefulness you can. Decide not just to remember, but to remember *until at least the end of the semester,* and you really will.

The second cue makes use of time and place. As nearly as possible, you should attempt to study the same subject at the same time in the same place each day. You'll soon find that when you get to that time and place, you're automatically in the subject groove. Train your brain to think French in study cubbie B of the library at 7:00 p.m. on Mondays, Wednesdays, and Fridays, and it will no longer take you twenty minutes to get in the mood for studying French. You'll save time and you'll also remember more of what you're studying.

For best results, review for tests during that regular time slot you've chosen, too. The review will really go quicker, and you'll retain more.

There's one more way you can use association to train your brain to think on cue. When you begin your studying or homework, don't plunge right in on the new work. Spend the first two minutes thinking about what you learned last time, and about how that fits into the course outline. (We hope you made an outline before your first class. See Learning Tip 1 if you didn't.) Two minutes of pre-thinking will activate all the right nerve endings for associating what you're about to study.

To make association pay off, you'll need a study timetable that you'll stick to. Most books on studying give detailed instructions for making a study-time schedule. We're sure that you already know how to make one. It's sticking to it that's hard.

Give yourself a break. Be realistic and flexible. Figure out how much time you *really* want to study, and break that time into logical segments for each course. Teachers would love to see two hours of study for every hour of class time, but in reality some subjects demand more time than others. You can't finalize a schedule until you're several weeks into the semester and have an idea of each course's demands on you.

One fact to keep in mind when scheduling is that, for most people, the brain works best during daylight hours. It's been found that each hour used for study during the day is as good as an hour and a half at night.

Don't get trapped into making an ideal schedule that you can't possibly follow. If you've never studied more than sixteen hours a week, don't suddenly try to lock yourself into thirty hours. You'll get better grades by giving yourself a realistic half hour for each subject, and sticking to that, than by scheduling an hour for each and throwing in the towel on *all* of it after five or six grueling weeks. Unlike Pavlov, it won't do you any good to prove that a person can salivate on cue if her head is chopped off.

REMEMBERING TIP 2
Eliminate Brain Interference

The brain is like a radio. Some people come equipped with automatic frequency control. They're the kind who can study in the middle of the *Rocky Horror Picture Show.*

Most of us aren't that lucky. We can't turn a switch in our heads and automatically tune out interference. We've got to work hard to concentrate. Our best recourse is to eliminate as many distractions as we can in advance.

Most distractions come in through our senses: sight, sound, touch, taste, smell. Eliminating most of them is easy if you think about it. If you study in your room, turn away from the window and close the door. Face a blank wall for best results. If you study in the library or student union, find a spot where people aren't constantly walking past the edge of your vision. Stay far from the smells of food, too.

If you're a nibbler, keep pretzels or small candies close at hand. That should eliminate interfering urges to think about what to eat. Try to avoid nervous habits like chewing fingernails or twisting your hair, too, or you'll end up thinking about the hair and nails and not about the subject you're studying. One good way to kick nervous fiddling is to keep a pencil or pen in hand and think about what notes you ought to take.

Everyone knows that the sounds of whispering friends are as distracting as a loud party. But few of us like to admit that background music is also interference. Dr. Mack T. Henderson proved through research that college people who usually study with music in the background study better when it's turned off. If you *must* have noise in your background, try a tape or record of white noise.

You can eliminate some more brain interference by organizing so that you have your study tools ready in advance. If you stop in the midst of working a sample math problem to figure out where you put the calculator, it's going to take several minutes after you find it to get your mind back in the right memory groove for math.

Some brain interference is caused by irrelevant things that we're trying to hold in our memories: test dates, deadlines, the time of the dance Saturday evening. Get things like this out of your head and onto paper so you won't have to fight against their interference. Keep a written calendar of deadlines, appointments, coming events, birthdays, and such. Tack up reminder lists of errands to do, letters to write, phone calls to make, questions you want to ask friends and teachers. Keep trivia like this on paper and it won't cause brain interference.

Emotional interference is hardest to counteract. If you're in love, you're going to find it hard to study. If you're in trouble, it'll be hard to keep other facts and ideas in your head. If you're angry at a teacher's unfairness, even that can interfere with remembering. Love is a great feeling you won't want to get rid of, but take some steps to solve your troubles and vent your angers so you can get them off your mind. If nothing else helps, see a school psychologist.

The only emotion that seems to help you remember better is anxiety. If you're anxious about passing a course, that could motivate you to remember better. But if it's a medical lab test you're anxious about, it's the wrong kind of anxiety when you're studying French. Only tension about the French course will help you remember French.

Brain interference also comes when you study similar subjects one after the other. That kind of interference can work backward and forward. If you study the declension for *go* in French and then, soon after, in Italian, learning the Italian verb forms can wipe out part of your memory of the French forms. Or what you learned in French can interfere now with remembering the Italian.

The more similar the kinds of learning taking place, the more back-and-forth interference you'll get. So when you make up your study schedule, separate two language courses with the study of history or chemistry, and separate physics and calculus with a course that doesn't involve remembering formulas.

How much time can you save if you cut out brain interference? A lot! One experiment moved students from a noisy, crowded room to a quiet study area—and shaved more than seven hours from their study time. In less than three hours, they accomplished as much as it had taken them ten hours to do before.

REMEMBERING TIP 3

Reinforce the Right Memories

If you have a really good memory, you're going to forget at least one-fourth of what you learn by the end of the day you learn it. If you're like most of us, count on forgetting a lot more than that. The only way to hold facts and thoughts in your head long enough to be tested on them is to keep reinforcing your impressions.

Scientists have figured out the most efficient schedule for long-term remembering: reinforce once five minutes after learning, once later the same day, once the next day, once the next week, once the next month, and once right before the test. We'll have more to say as we go along about how to do each reinforcement painlessly.

But do make sure you reinforce only correct information. Before you turn on the memory circuits each time, check with your notes to be sure you've got the facts and ideas right. If you've read Learning Tip 11, you already know why this is very important.

Be especially wary of misremembering when you're trying to recall small details. The mind is a storyteller; it likes to fill in "facts" when it doesn't have them, and some of those mismemories seem as plausible as the true facts. Be sure to double-check any details that you've worked hard to dredge up from your memory *before* you reinforce them in your brain.

For the same reason, correct misinformation and misunderstanding as soon as you know about it. When you do homework, rework your wrong answers. Straighten out errors as soon as you can. This is even true of practicing a musical instrument. If you've ever memorized a musical composition and played it in public, you know that most of the parts you stumbled over were the parts you got wrong the first, second, and third time through and never quite corrected. You never did erase the faulty connection.

Use every chance you have to pinpoint places where your thinking is faulty. If the instructor gives frequent quizzes, you're in luck. But many college courses have only a midterm and a final. For those, be smart—find a workbook that has answers in the back, and test yourself periodically. If you can check your accuracy, it's been shown your self-confidence will actually speed up your memory.

REMEMBERING TIP 4

Roll with Your Alertness Cycles

The amount of *attention* you give a subject is as important as the amount of *time* you spend. The more alert you are while studying, the more you'll learn.

Since alertness diminishes from the time we begin a task to the time we end it, divide your study schedule so that you tackle hard or boring subjects while you're at your most alert. Save the easy and more entertaining study for later on, when your enthusiasm will keep you from falling asleep.

We all go through two kinds of alertness cycles every day. The larger cycle determines whether we're "day" people or "night" people. Some of us take forever to get moving in the morning and get a good second wind after dinner that lasts long into the night. Most of the rest of us wake up early in the morning full of energy, but by nightfall we're not good for much brainwork. Knowing which type you are can help you decide when it's best for you to study. If you're a day person, you may get a lot more accomplished in a lot less time if you study before classes begin than if you try to concentrate in the evening. If you're a night person, evening study makes sense.

In addition to this large wake-sleep cycle, we all have smaller swings from alertness to fatigue and back, all during the day. Some scientists say these swings occur every two or three hours. Sometimes they last for just a minute or two, sometimes for a half hour or more. In some of us these swings are more noticeable than in others.

The important thing is to keep from trying to study right through these small fatigue periods. You'll probably remember very little afterward. But don't go to sleep either, unless you're the kind who wakes refreshed after a three-minute catnap. Instead, do something physical or interactive. Jog around the block or strum your guitar or clean up your desk or talk to your roommate or sort your notes. If you regularly fade out from 4:00 p.m. to 4:30 p.m., you could schedule that time to study with a friend.

There's another kind of alertness cycle that we ought to be aware of when we're trying to study. That's the cycle that makes us remember the beginning and end of any sustained-attention-span activity more than the part in the middle. When reviewing, mix up what you studied yesterday or last week so that the middle becomes the beginning or end.

One way to enhance your memory of what's in the middle is to tell it to yourself out loud as you go along. Repeating anything just once in your own voice increases the amount you remember by between 25 percent and 100 percent.

REMEMBERING TIP 5

Make Sleep Work for You

About a dozen years ago there was a rash of experiments in which people went to sleep with tape recorders plugged into their ears. The experimenters were out to prove that people could learn in their sleep.

They failed. People can't learn anything new when they're asleep—or even while they're falling asleep. If you conk out reading a novel, you probably won't be able to remember what you read during the half-awake state.

But there's a big difference between learning and remembering—and sleep does help you *remember* better. There are two forces at work in your favor.

First of all, there's the corollary of the interference factor we discussed in Remembering Tip 2. We said that the more interference you have, the harder it is to remember what you are learning. The opposite is just as true. The less interference you have to counteract, the more easily you'll remember—and the least brain interference of all comes when you're asleep.

So make sleep work for you. If you've got a test the next day, review your facts and ideas one last time while you're still alert, but after you've studied everything else. Close your books and get ready for bed, and your brain will keep on reinforcing your memories all through the night.

Research even tells us how long we ought to sleep for the best memory the next morning—at least four hours and preferably six. So if you stay up cramming until dawn for a 9:00 a.m. exam, you're probably cheating yourself out of your best grade. Moreover, between study and exam, you needn't rush right off to bed. Just do something relaxing with your mind. If you study early in the day, go to a movie, attend a party, and then crawl into the sack, you perform just as well—sometimes even better—than when you cram until bedtime.

But there's one more effect of sleep to take into account: sleeping just *before* you learn something new interferes with remembering, whether the sleep is a 30-minute nap or a full night's rest. It seems that you've got to get your brain fully awake before it agrees to process any new information.

Get to know yourself. Determine whether you wake up quickly or whether you're the kind who takes two hours to get going in the morning. If you're the latter kind, don't study first thing in the morning, and try to arrange your class schedule so that your early-morning classes don't call for heavy brainwork.

REMEMBERING TIP 6

Space Out Your Practice Times

Since your subconscious pitches in to help reinforce your memory between study sessions while you're asleep and while you're doing other things, take advantage of it. Space out practice times so that, in between, your subconscious keeps working. It takes no extra effort at all to get the benefit of subconscious reinforcement.

Another element that makes spaced practice doubly effective is called the Zeigarnik effect after its discoverer. According to the Zeigarnik effect, the brain tends to keep remembering things that it hasn't finished with, and tends to forget—at least consciously—things it is convinced it won't need to remember anymore. It is this quality that makes it hard for us to remember any of those dates we knew cold for last year's exam. That's why we told you in Remembering Tip 1 to study with the intention of remembering for a long time.

The great thing for students about the way the mind keeps remembering on its own is that you can sneak in some totally painless study while eating or running or dancing.

Left to its own devices, the mind chooses an interesting problem to keep working on. For most of us, the subjects that are interesting are the ones we are doing best in. To trick your mind into working on a hard topic, start it on the right track. Take a minute or two—at the dance or on the court—to consciously focus on the ideas or facts that you would like reinforced.

As with all free benefits in life, there's a point of diminishing return. If you space out your reviews *too* much, you begin to forget. For most subjects and most people, the ideal spacing is as follows:

1st review: five to ten minutes after learning
2nd review: later the same day
3rd review: one week later
4th review: one month later
5th review: just before the exam

Your ideal spacing may be smaller or greater. For subjects that are difficult or boring, you may need up to twice as many reviews. (That's one reason we suggested that you play it smart and work up as much enthusiasm as you can from the beginning.) The more memory work in a course, the more practice you need, too.

To take further advantage of spaced-out reinforcement, break up your final test review time into two periods. First, study during the evening before the exam. (But stop as soon as alertness fades. You'll start messing up your brain signals if you try to remember when you're overtired.) Then reinforce your memory once more, briefly, after you wake up.

How do you get that first review, the one that comes five or ten minutes after learning? If it's out-of-class learning, it's easy. Just close the book, get some soda or a candy bar, or take some other short break. (Keep it short!) Then sit down and *write* everything you're supposed to remember: summary, names, dates, rules, what-have-you. (*This* is the time to write those textbook chapter notes we talked about in Learning Tips 5 and 9.) Once you've got them down, check back to make sure that your memory is correct.

In this case, the second review should be a fast checklist review of each subject's main ideas just before you close shop for the night. Five minutes' attention to each subject is sufficient.

If you're reviewing classroom learning, grab the time for it while you're heading for your next class: do a mental review of the main points. (But leave yourself five minutes to *preview*—to get your head in the right frame of reference for the lecture that is coming up next.) For your second review, in the evening, read your class notes and develop your clue words. (See Learning Tip 9.)

A two-minute review of yesterday's material, at the beginning of today's lecture or homework assignment, is an alternate way to get the second review time in. (In Remembering Tip 9 we will suggest many ways to review.) All along, it's important to test your memory—to see how much you can recall without referring to previous notes—and then to check your memory to make sure it is accurate. But do not dally, or you'll get bored. Push your brain right along. Consider it practice for racing the clock on your next exam.

REMEMBERING TIP 7

Make Your Muscles Do the Remembering

Students spend countless hours trying to get facts into their heads, thinking that that's where all the remembering occurs. But our muscles really have better memories than our heads. We once watched while a 68-year-old man climbed on a bike for the first time after forty years and, after a few tentative pedalings, was balancing as well as you or we could. Though his brain was able to recall less than 10 percent of all the facts he had learned during his first twenty-eight years, his muscles remembered about 90 percent of what they had learned.

That's why just the act of taking notes—even if you never look at those notes again—will get you higher marks on a test than just listening. Note-taking is a muscle activity. (Typing, unfortunately, doesn't make for muscle memory unless you can type your test.)

Some students cannot listen well while they're taking notes. If the lecturer provides course notes, or if they can be bought on campus, these crutches are good for such students. But if *you* use them, the best way to remember is to rewrite them, changing the words as much as you can without changing the meaning. To change them around, you'll have to think about what you're writing, and your muscle memory will be reinforced.

You may think you're missing a lot of information by taking notes during lectures. But experiments show that you miss a lot more if you listen and then, after the lecture, try to remember what was said and then write it down . . . or if you follow along with someone else's notes, no matter how thorough. Research convinces us that you remember a lot more if your muscles' write it down.

REMEMBERING TIP 8
See and Say

Back in grade school, we all had show-and-tell. Besides being fun, teacher knew it helped us to remember. That's because it combines two big memory prods: sight and sound. If we can tie visual images to things we want to remember, we remember them better. (Try it: without looking back, see if you can remember what idea the image of old-man-on-the-bicycle demonstrated in the previous tip.) If we *hear* someone explain an idea to us, that too helps us remember it.

So make use of sight and sound to help yourself remember. Make the diagrams and other visual depictions of your study material that are shown in Learning Tip 9. Learn, too, to make tangible pictures in your mind to remind you of the ideas and facts you want to remember. For example, to remember the date the Industrial Revolution began, you could picture an appropriate scene from Dickens or *City Lights* or even the movie *Norma Rae* and carve the date, in your head, on a machine in the picture. (Visual imagery like this is the secret behind some of the memory feats of great magicians.)

To get sound working for you, talk over your coursework with a friend. When you're studying a foreign language, it is particularly helpful to say the words aloud. In class, say them along with the teacher or student who is reciting. While studying, tell them to yourself. When you read a chapter, summarize its parts, bit by bit, out loud as you go along. Explain it to yourself. Tell yourself how it connects to what you read before, and listen to yourself talk. (If you're self-conscious, do this type of study alone.)

Combine see and say techniques. Tell yourself the visual image you have created to remember a particular fact or idea. Then combine auditory and visual memory with muscle memory: as you write, say the words aloud. As you make a diagram, tell yourself what the connections are. Get all three memory devices working together, and you'll end up with more than triple the benefit.

REMEMBERING TIP 9

Never Study Anything the Same Way Twice

We know that this tip is almost impossible to follow. Sooner or later, for any one topic, you're going to run out of alternatives and have to repeat one of your study methods. But don't give up without a fight. Try to be as inventive as you can, because each different way you process an idea or fact makes a different association for it. Storage in your long-term memory is only of value if you can retrieve all the data when you need it from your memory bank. The more paths you have in your head to any piece of information, the more likely you are going to find one of the paths to it even when you're tired and anxious and distracted in the exam room.

We'll list some of the many ways we have found to study. They make use of our sight, sound, and muscle memory cells.

(1) Study your notes by finding a different logical order and then rewriting them in that order.

(2) Pick out key words from your notes and write them.

(3) Once you have key words next to your notes (if you've followed Learning Tip 9), shift your looseleaf pages around so that they're in an order that makes the most sense for studying. Take the first page and cover up the notes portion, leaving just the clues visible. See if you can remember the notes that go with the clues.

(4) Mix up the order of your notes—or of your key words—and test whether you can remember facts and ideas out of order. (For short-answer tests, this is excellent preparation, since you are going to have to recall facts and catchwords out of context.)

(5) Study what is in the textbook, too, by assigning your notes clue words. Test whether you associate the clue word with the longer note that it refers to.

(6) Associate your clue words with images. Describe each image aloud. Draw a sketch of the image and tell yourself how the sketch connects with the complete idea or fact. (You needn't be an artist. You're the only one who has to recognize the sketch.) If you cannot make a sketch, make a word diagram, table, graph, or whatever visual representation you can think or. For instance, the best way to remember a great many aspects of the relationship between Athens and Troy is to draw a map pinpointing them in the Mediterranean environment.

(7) Associate ideas with one another by forming links you'll remember. The best links are visual. For instance, to tie Planck with the quantum theory, we visualize crackling bundles of energy teetering on a plank.

(8) Reword ideas and facts. Explain to yourself what they mean. For instance, one textbook tells us that an algorithm is a sequence of steps that can be taken to solve all problems of a particular type. We've reworded it: an algorithm is all the steps that go toward solving all problems of the same type. (We inserted *all* and *go* in our rewording to help us remember. If you can add a trick or joke in your rewording, it's a helpful memory prod.)

(9) Group facts and ideas into categories that make sense to you. Try to keep your groups to fewer than seven items in a category. People can remember up to seven things in one bundle; more than that and they may get confused.

(10) When you study grouped words, look for a rhythm to the list. Your memory of the rhythm will help you fill in missing words. For example, the following are all Italian Renaissance authors:

Dante, Petrarch, Boccaccio, Machiavelli, Castiglione, Cellini.

If we had to remember their names, we'd create a stronger rhythm—and even a little rhyme—that helps:

Dante, Castiglione, Cellini, Machiavelli, Petrarch, and Boccaccio.

Be as imaginative as you like in dreaming up new ways to run your study material through your brain. Each new way will get you that much closer to an A.

REMEMBERING TIP 10

Keep Each Study Session Short

For any one course, do your studying in short takes. You'll remember more after four one-hour sessions distributed over four days than after one marathon six-hour stint.

For textbook reading and note studying, your best time-span is about fifty minutes a course. If you're doing straight memorization, whether math formulas or a foreign language or names and dates, twenty to thirty minutes' time is plenty. That's because you cram in more information when you are rote memorizing than with the other kinds of memory work. Don't try to remember 100 percent all at once, either. Build up your memory little by little. If you remember half your list of conjugations today, pat yourself on the back, put your notes away, and try for a higher number tomorrow.

One reason you learn better in short takes is that you use time more efficiently when you're under an imposed time restriction. (Have you noticed how many facts and figures you manage to cram in the day before a big exam?) Another reason is that you're letting your mind do some subconscious work on its own between your study times. (We explained all about this reinforcement value in Remembering Tip 6.) But the most important reason is that your brain gets tired and loses interest after you spend a long time on one subject. Unless you are alert and involved, you'll remember very little for any length of time.

Two kinds of study situations are exceptions to the keep-it-short rule. One is library research. There, you're moving around and constantly shifting from one book or paper to another. There's enough change of pace to keep you alert for at least several hours.

The other exception is writing a paper. If you stick to the fifty-minute rule, you'll just about have your notes organized and your outline constructed when you'll be forced to pack it in. But that's the point when your brain is teeming with its utmost inspiration. Start writing, and don't stop until you're at least a few pages into the first draft. Then, if you run out of steam, stop for the day. Let your thoughts percolate around in your subconscious. When you pick up next time, copy the last page or so that you've written just to put your mind in the right groove again. In most cases, you will find that the rest of the paper moves along surprisingly easily.

REMEMBERING TIP 11

Make Time for Study Breaks

The specialists say you'll do your most effective studying if you take a ten-minute break between subjects. It helps three ways.

(1) It's a part of behavior modification. Pavlov's dogs remembered to respond on cue by being rewarded with tidbits. Think of each break as your reward for putting in fifty minutes of studying effort.

(2) It acts just like a brief sleep. If you don't do anything brainy during the ten minutes, you'll get some free reinforcement of your learning.

(3) It keeps brain-wave interference at a minimum, by separating the two subjects very clearly in your mind.

Don't be rigid about taking breaks only between subjects, however, or you'll end up watching the clock more than the books. If you feel the urge to get up and move around for a few minutes, do it. Don't *overdo* it: if you get too many urges, one antidote that works for some is to set your alarm and forget it. Then you'll hold down the breaks without needing to clock-watch.

One good time to take a short break—no longer than five minutes at most—is right after reading your textbook assignment. Wait until *after* the break to write down the summary or notes. This procedure will guarantee that you'll remember more of what you have read, for longer, and it will make more sense.

REMEMBERING TIP 12

Keep Squeezing Your Notes

Once you've done the *learning* on your coursework—the part of your brainwork that enables you to understand it—the only thing that will help you remember it long enough to do well in the end-term exam is to keep reviewing it on the schedule we've suggested (see Remembering Tip 1). The trouble is, if you reviewed *all* your notes for *every* course at least five times through, by the end of the semester you'd be spending a monumental amount of time on review.

The smartest students keep compressing their notes into smaller and smaller size. As they understand relationships between one week's work and the next, they consolidate and organize. By the end of the course, they can tell you most of the main ideas, subordinate ideas, definitions, and examples just by consulting a few pages or 3 × 5 cards. This constant consolidation works in nearly every course, and it pays off in big dividends.

As you review, keep squeezing your own notes. Play with the material as we suggested in Remembering Tip 9: organize it into charts, formulas, or other short-form arrangements. Having to organize and compress will force you to see the relationships between ideas that get people A's on exams. It will help you to focus on the big picture that's more important, in writing an essay, than all the little details and facts. (Knowing the facts and details only raises your essay grades if you know what statements they support.) If you compress the path of the Industrial Revolution on a chart, you may suddenly discover that the canning industry (page 45 of your notes) was exempt from child labor laws (page 24)—a point that neither instructor nor textbook bothered to make in so many words.

Whenever you discover relationships in your notes, think about them and see if you can draw some inferences or conclusions of your own from them. (In this case, was it because the cannery owners were a powerful group of lobbyists?) Being able to draw independent conclusions from the facts automatically earns a better grade.

Once a week, consolidate that week's notes. This will serve as your one-week review. Once a month, squeeze the four weeks' notes into one or two pages of clue words and patterns, for a good one-month review. Then, before each big exam, do a final organization and consolidation. Make sure, as you go, that your notes are completely accurate. Don't trust your memory, but check facts carefully between one set of notes and the next. After you have your notes consolidated, each time, check your memory. Make sure that you remember correctly what the cue word, formula, or main idea you've written down is supposed to stand for. Make sure that what you leave out, as you compress, is firmly associated with your compressed note in your memory. By the end of the term, when you see $E \cong mc^2$, you should be able to rattle off the definition, derivation, history, uses, and whatever else your instructor expects you to be responsible for in connection with the equation. Your associative memory will be working right on cue.

REMEMBERING TIP 13

Keep Memorizing to a Minimum

Most students memorize a great deal. The fact is, straight memorizing is the *least* dependable way to remember anything.

When we learn something, we store it as a dent on the brain. To retrieve it—remember it—we've got to find a path to it. If we associate it with something else, that's one path. The more associations we can set up, the more paths, and the easier it is to remember.

But if we memorize a thing, all we do is make a deeper dent. We don't set up any paths at all. We can recite the number .000548 until it is burned on our brains, but unless we associate it with the mass of an electron particle, we have no way of retrieving the number when we want it except by chance.

We rarely memorize anything without *one* association. In this case we would all have thought of the electron particle along with its .000548 mass as we memorized it. But you will remember a lot faster—and better—if you set up several associations, not just one. In fact, for every association you add to your memorization, you're that much better off.

Here's a handy list of ways you can keep straight memorizing to a minimum. (We repeat some previously discussed ways so that you've got them here for ready reference.)

(1) *Associate.* Link it to something you do remember. For most courses, patterning sets up associations for us. Catchwords and key phrases help us associate ideas. Associations of personal significance make strong links, too. For example, the 548 in an electron's mass is the number of letter's in Frank's name: Frank(5)lynn(4) Peterson(8); and the three zeros are the three groups of words in his name.

(2) *Visualize.* Make a picture on your mind's eye. The sillier or stranger the picture, the better you'll remember the idea. This game works especially well in memorizing foreign words. In fact, it will give you a native's ability to recall the word without having to translate first into English.

Here's an example: *carte,* the French word for *map.* Our mind's eye pictures a map of the Congo, held by an explorer who's barking to his equipment porters, "Cart(e), cart(e), cart(e)."

(3) *Sound out.* Say it aloud and listen to its sound. Have you ever had a word on the tip of your tongue, and hunted around in your head for its sound? Then you'll recognize what an important part sound plays in helping us remember.

Group words and listen to their rhyme and rhythm. This also reinforces sound memory. Here's an example: An electron's *weight* is point-o-o-o-5-4-8.

(4) *Count.* If you need to remember the causes of the Crimean War, it helps if you know that your notes contain *four* causes. If your memory hunt supplies only three, you'll know that there's a fourth cause lurking in your subconscious.

Our minds seem to have much less trouble remembering the *number* of key words we've listed under any main topic than the key words themselves. Learn the number, and it will be a valuable memory clue.

(5) *Abbreviate.* The mind's eye recalls short blocks of capital letters more quickly than several long words. Link together OPEC and the FTC in your mind when you're studying, instead of trying to remember that there's a tie between the Organization of Petroleum Export Countries and the Federal Trade Commission. (But do make sure that you know what your abbreviations stand for.)

Acronyms are abbreviations that we create ourselves to help us remember. Usually they're the first letters of a bunch of key words. One example is OK4R, which reminds us of the reading system described in Learning Tip 5: *O*verview, *K*ey words, *R*ead, *R*ite, *R*ecite, *R*eview. To remember the ten lightest physical elements, you could try:

HHeLiBeB CNOFNe (pronounced H-Helibeb Cnofne)

Other mnemonics—memory cues—consist of turning first letters into words that, strung together, make some sense. One example is Every Good Boy Does Fine, which is used to remember the names of the musical notes on the lines of the treble clef.

Formulas are abbreviations, too. The funnier they look, the more *sight* will help us remember them. But it won't do any good to memorize that $E \cong mc^2$ unless we remember what E, m, and c stand for. In fact, for a science, math, or other technical course, the best way to remember is to actually understand how to derive the formula. Then, if your rote memory fails, you can find it by association. (Of course, some formulas are basic definitions; they can't be derived from anything else.)

Some things do have to be memorized primarily by rote: a poem or a part in a play, for example. But there, too, you should also make as much use as you can of logical association. First find key words in the passage, then search for a relationship that leads you from one to the next. These stops will help your memory along.

Unless a passage is very long, try to memorize it all at once instead of breaking it up into pieces. If you must learn it piecemeal, keep the chunks as big as possible, and work hardest on learning the links between the chunks. They're always the least-learned parts. It may seem quicker to you to try to remember a little at a time, but researchers have shown that it really is faster the other way. This is true for rote memorizing of musical compositions as well as verbal pieces.

Repeat the fact or idea or passage until you know it cold—and then wait five minutes and repeat it a few times more. That's called *overlearning*. Dumb people associate it with *overwork*. Smart folks know that it's more akin to *overpowering*: defeating the test with your superior force.

When you're sharpening your memory, whether it's formulas or concepts you're studying, *first* try to remember and *then* check your notes. Even if you are sure you're right, do check. If a mismemory has crept in, it should be corrected as fast as possible.

Learning is just a matter of understanding; it's only hard if you're dealing with a difficult concept. But remembering takes work whether the item is hard or easy. In fact, we tend to remember hard things longer than easier ones, simply because we work harder at it.

One way to speed up the retention process is to keep in your head the idea or fact you want to remember for at least a few seconds so that it has time to make a strong enough impression. Scientists found that lab rats must keep a thought in the brain for ninety seconds in order to remember it long-term. For people, they think, holding time should be about five seconds. One good way to hold the idea is to play with it in one of the ways we've suggested in this section and in Remembering Tip 9. And while you are holding the thought you want to remember, don't let your mind stray to your stomach's needs.

There is one final key to remembering: confidence. If you think that you're going to forget a key formula or phrase, you can bet *that* thought will interfere directly with the phrase you're trying to remember. Relax. Assume that you will remember. Let the associations, images, and abbreviations roll. You'll remember better than you ever could before.

REMEMBERING TIP 14

Let Your Written Homework Do Your Reviewing

Written homework can be attacked in two ways. One is to race through it as fast as you can, with one eye on the clock and the other out the window. That's the way most of us have been doing it since grade school.

But a few smart students have figured out—though nobody bothers to tell them—that written assignments are supposed to help a person review. If you work up some interest in doing them, so that you can really give them your attention, they provide both a check on whether you've learned everything correctly, and the muscle-and-sight practice that imbeds the learning in your brain and makes the memory connections.

To get the most benefit from written homework, first figure out what information or ideas it is designed to help you remember. Then make sure that you understand all those concepts and facts *before* you start writing.

Math and science problems are usually devised to help you remember concepts, laws, formulas, and new words. Don't keep looking back and copying facts and equations, and don't just plug the problem's numbers into the textbook or blackboard sample. You defeat the point of the homework; you just waste your own precious time. Keep in mind that each problem is really a memory-training exercise. Do one from memory, then look back and check if you're unsure, and then do the next from memory too. With difficult or tricky concepts, it's a good idea to attempt the sample problem from memory and then check it against the book before you do the first homework problem. That way, you'll have an immediate check on whether you understand each step.

If you can't do a problem that has complex numbers in it, try substituting simple numbers before you look back. Isolate whether it's the idea you're stuck on, or just the arithmetic.

Check all your results, if you can, and do over any problems you got wrong. If your book doesn't contain answers, inspect your answers to see if they seem logically correct. Keep in mind that, in technical subjects, you learn infinitely more from your mistakes than from your correct answers, so long as you take the time to pinpoint the places that have given you trouble and then correct your misconceptions and mislearned facts.

Researchers have found that doing a hundred problems doesn't "train" you to get the correct answer in the hundred-and-first. All you can expect of problems is reinforcement of your memory of the equation and the method of solution—so long as you use your memory and don't simply copy.

Some experts advise that you read each math or science problem through *twice* before you begin it, to make sure that you know exactly what's being asked for. Then jot down what's *given,* what's to be *proved,* and the *principle* or *law* that's to be used. Whenever you can, make a *diagram* that helps you see the problem. In your second reading, circle or jot down every important piece of information including the unit of measurement for each number.

Because each new math and science fact and idea tends to build on others before it, keeping up with your homework and doing it correctly will provide you with automatic, painless reviews. But if you get behind in your learning, or you keep looking up applicable data without prodding your memory to dredge it up for homework assignments, you'll cheat yourself of a lot of free, valuable memory training.

Language homework is just as valuable. Its purpose is to help you review all the words and phrases you've learned up to that point. It is usually divided into two parts: reading for general comprehension, and writing for specific translation.

Each assignment can add between twenty and fifty new words—a great deal if you try to memorize it all using straight rote memorization.

So cut down on rote memorizing. Make use of the other remembering devices. Use association: let the context help you figure out the meaning, if it's general comprehension you're after. Read the passage through quickly several times (out loud, to review using sound and sight cues), even the words you don't understand. By the third time you read, you will have figured out a number of them. The third time through, pencil a question mark next to the words you still don't know; after you've finished the passage, go back and look them up.

Now call on muscle memory. Write down each question-marked word on a separate card, and on the other side write the meaning. You can tote the cards around and study the words at your leisure, stashing away each card as you've learned the word. (Pull out the cards once after a week, and then once a month to review, and then one last time to study at exam time.)

To learn the new words and phrases on your cards, call on association whenever you can. The *best* way to learn is to use each new word in conversation three times during a day. (That's why the Berlitz intensive method—where you live, eat, and breathe the language all day every day for several weeks—is so effective.) You can get extra practice, painlessly and with no extra time involved, if you keep one step ahead of the class in your homework. Then, if you think and whisper along with the instructor or whoever's reciting, your class time will become a very effective review hour.

We'll repeat what we said once before about learning a foreign language: done well, it is intensive, hard work. Keep your homework times short—a half hour or less—and break them up with dinner, relaxation, or studying that uses a different part of your brain.

English and social studies homework often consist of

writing essays. Here, too, it's important to isolate the point of the assignment. Usually the goal is a review of some important idea or principle. Read the assignment carefully, and determine what's being asked for. The following terms usually have the following specific meanings, though there's always an instructor who means something else by them.

Name, list, tell, and *enumerate* all mean to give just the information that's specifically asked for.

Summarize and *outline* mean give the main points.

Define means just give the meaning.

Illustrate means give examples.

Justify means give the facts that prove it is true.

Prove means show that it is true and that its opposite is false.

Discuss and *review* mean examine from all angles.

Compare means show how they are the same and how they differ.

Contrast means just show how they differ.

Evaluate means give your opinion as to the advantages and disadvantages.

Criticize means examine the pros and cons and give your judgment.

Explain means show, in logical sequence, how or why something happened (or both).

These are all words that help you decide what kind of paper is called for, and the point of view that you are being asked to take. But keep your eye firmly on the essay *subject*—the idea or principle that you are being asked to develop in one of the preceding ways. Do not wander off onto a topic that you know better or feel more comfortable with; most paper-graders lower your mark for that.

If something unforseen pulls you behind in a course, try to at least skim the assignments. Then soak up as much learning and review as you can in class. If you're behind, it's even more imperative than otherwise *not* to cut class.

REMEMBERING TIP 15

Talk It Through with a Study Group

The Paper Chase has made every one of us wonder if learning and remembering could both be done best by forming a study group. The answer is yes, no, and maybe. It depends on the group, and on how much each person relies on the group, and for what.

The difference between a study group and a tutorial situation is this: a tutor is someone who can be relied on to know what she's talking about. Any explanations and information you get from her are guaranteed by the tutor's sponsoring group or recommender (the department? the study skills center?) to be accurate. The students in a study group, on the other hand, are all learning the material at the same time. Some are better students, but they don't necessarily have the correct answers. If you rely on study group members for information, you may be sorry. You can't depend on their answers to anything. So for best results, here's how to use a study group.

(1) *When:* Join a study group *after* you've learned the facts and ideas that you need to know. That way, you won't learn incorrect information.

(2) *Why:* The purpose of the group should be *conversation*—to help you exercise your sight and sound senses and your mouth muscles in reviewing so that you'll remember long-term. If you sit back and listen to the others, you'll get one benefit out of three. If *you* tell what you know to the others, you'll benefit three ways. (You'll also learn better by having to explain your ideas in coherent terms. Remember, tests show that the tutor learns as much as the tutee!)

(3) *How:* Any method that will get you thinking and

talking about your ideas and the facts you've learned is a good method. If it's ideas you're studying, ask each other questions that could be on an essay exam. In fact, one very effective technique is for each member to prepare five essay questions in advance, and then for the group to take turns answering them all.

If your group needs to work on memorization of facts, drill one another with clue words.

(4) *Where:* Choose a place where there are no distractions, so that the group can give its entire attention to the subject. And choose someplace where group enthusiasm won't be dampened by someone saying, "Tone it down," in the background.

(5) *How long:* An advantage of study groups is that they often make even a dull subject interesting. That will help your memory. On the other hand, there's a tendency to sidetrack into talk about dates or football scores. One hour spent with everyone's mind on the subject is worth four hours' work with time-outs every few minutes for fun and games.

(6) *Who:* Anyone—just so long as he or she understands the point of the study group: not to teach but to discuss facts and ideas that are already learned; not to socialize, but to study. Study groups help slow students put together relationships between facts. They help bright students realize that test-preparers like straightforward answers. They help inarticulate or shy students become more articulate. They help everyone prepare for class discussion, when discussion is an important part of the grade.

Study groups, viewers of *The Paper Chase* can tell you, are great when it comes to preparing for oral tests. But for written exams (especially short-answer tests), written review is still best.

REMEMBERING TIP 16

Make Cramming Pay Off

There are two kinds of cramming. In the first kind, you begin—about three days before the big test—to start learning the coursework. You do all the reading, make a pile of notes, and try to memorize like crazy until you've got it all crammed into your brain. If you're a good crammer, everything you need to know sticks right at the top of your head, where—if you don't get so anxious that you forget it all—it will last just long enough. The morning after the test, you'll wake up to find that not more than 20 percent of what you learned is still remembered. The rest hasn't percolated through to your long-term memory.

If you like standing on the edge of precipices, you can cram like this for any course where you're convinced you'll never need any of the knowledge again. (We *do* wonder why, at today's tuition rates, you took the course in the first place.) For all other courses, there's a better way. If you've followed our tips until here, cramming for any big exam should take no more than three or four hours, and should result in a high grade.

If you've reviewed actively, by now you should have a couple of pages, at most, of condensed clue words, lists, charts, and diagrams that represent all the main ideas and facts that you need to know for the course—and that activate your brain to fill in remembered details. For foreign languages, you'll have the word and phrase cards you made, as well as a list of regular verbs and charts of irregular verbs, organized according to the pattern of endings they fit into. For technical courses, you may have formula cards with their derivations on the back, and cards with equivalents that you've had to memorize by rote.

Spend the first hour or so for each course organizing the above condensed notes. Then pull out the course outline you began with at the beginning of the semester, and reread it. This will help put your notes in perspective, clarify the logical units into which they divide, and clue you further on the relative importance of all the information you've learned.

Take another hour or so to rewrite your notes, trying actively to reorganize and condense them even further so that they make the most sense. Check your memory as you go, and leave out every fact and subordinate idea that you already know cold. After you're done, you should have a page or two of main topics and memory prods.

While that final review sinks in, shift gears for a few minutes. Try to guess what the test is likely to be like. Will it be short answer, essay, or a combination? Will it be machine-scored or corrected by a live body—and if so, whose? (A teaching assistant with an answer sheet may not recognize a correct answer said in words the professor hasn't used.) Also decide what type of information you'll be asked to provide. If it's short-answer (also called objective testing), you won't have to do any deep thinking. You'll just need to be able to *recognize* correct answers, which is a lot easier than having to *recall* them. As a rule, you won't need to remember your coursework as completely as if you were writing essays.

For essay exams, prepare by selecting 8 or 10 main topics, based on the units in the course, and make up one or two questions having to do with each topic. (An easy way is to tack on a word or two from the list in Remembering Tip 14; for example, *compare* and *contrast* the *X main topic* to the *Y main topic*.) Then jot down the outline you would follow in writing each essay. Don't bother to write any of the essays unless you want practice in composition.

For oral exams, prepare in exactly the same way as for essays. In terms of needed information, there is not much difference between them.

One researcher suggests the following guide to help you figure out what's expected of you on essay tests. Don't treat it as gospel; your teacher may expect more or less of you. No matter how little time you're given, count on spending half your time recalling and organizing your answer, and the other half on the actual writing.

Time allotted per essay question	*Total words expected per essay question*	*Number of details to give for each main point*
2 to 5 minutes	20 to 30 words	none
10 to 15 minutes	50 to 75 words	1 for each
20 to 30 minutes	100 to 150 words	2 for each
45 to 60 minutes	300 to 500 words	3 for each

To prepare for exams in which you'll have to solve problems, copy one advanced problem from the textbook (if it supplies answers) or from past homework assignments for each important principle or law that you're responsible for knowing. (Usually, authors arrange problem sets in order of difficulty, so choose one toward the end of the group.) Then mix up the problems so that you can test whether you recognize them out of context and out of order. Solve them, and check them against the correct answers. You'll know very quickly just where your weak spots are.

This kind of cramming, combined with our other study tips, is short, efficient, and productive. It won't guarantee you an A on the exam. You've also got to know how to take a test—which is an entire book's worth of knowledge right there. (In fact, our companion book, *Test-Taking Strategies,* does cover everything you need to know about it.)

But the tips you've read, which are all based on the latest scientific research, do promise a higher grade than you've ever gotten before.

APPENDIX

HELPFUL BOOKS

Buzan, Tony, *Use Both Sides of Your Brain* (E. P. Dutton, 1976).

Furst, Bruno, *Stop Forgetting* (Doubleday & Company, Inc., 1979).

Kesselman-Turkel, Judi, and Peterson, Franklynn, *Good Writing* (Franklin Watts, 1981).

Kesselman-Turkel, Judi, and Peterson, Franklynn, *Test-Taking Strategies* (Contemporary Books, Inc., 1981).

McCormick, Mona, *The New York Times Guide to Reference Materials* (Popular Library, 1978).

Norman, Maxwell H., *Successful Reading: Key to Our Dynamic Society* (Holt, Rinehart and Winston, 1968). Note: describes OARWET note-taking technique.

Pauk, Walter, *How to Study in College* (Houghton Mifflin, second edition, 1970). Note: describes OK4R note-taking technique.

Rivers, William L., *Finding Facts* (Prentice Hall, 1975).

Robinson, Francis P., *Effective Study* (Harper and Row, revised edition, 1970). Note: describes SQ3R note-taking technique.

Sprache, George D., and Berg, Paul C., *The Art of Efficient Reading* (The Macmillan Company, 1966). Note: describes PQRST note-taking technique.

Todd, Alden, *Finding Facts Fast* (Ten Speed Press, second edition, 1980).

Weinland, James D., *How to Improve Your Memory* (Barnes and Noble, 1957).

TECHNICAL PAPERS OF INTEREST

Eanet, Marilyn G., and Manzo, Anthony V., "REAP—A Strategy for Improving Reading/Writing/Study Skills," (*Journal of Reading,* May 1976, pp. 647–652).

Edwards, Peter, "Panorama: A Study Technique" (*Journal of Reading,* November 1973, pp. 132–135).

Hanf, M. Buckley, "Mapping: A Technique for Translating Reading into Thinking" (*Journal of Reading,* January 1971, pp. 225–230, 270).

Lin, Herbert, "Effective Study of Physics: Tips for the Beginning Student" (*The Physics Teacher,* April 1979, pp. 243–245).

Palmatier, Robert and Bennett, J. Michael, "Note-Taking Habits of College Students" (*Journal of Reading,* December 1974, pp. 215–218).

Palmatier, Robert, "A Note-Taking System for Learning," (*Journal of Reading,* October 1973, pp. 36–39).

Policastro, Michael, "Note-Taking: The Key to College Success" (*Journal of Reading,* February 1975, pp. 372–375).

Richards, John P., "Note-Taking, Underlining, Inserted Questions, and Organizers in Text: Research Conclusions and Educational Implications" (*Educational Technology,* June 1980, pp. 5–11).

Solon, Carol, "The Pyramid Diagram: A College Study Skills Tool" (*Journal of Reading,* April 1980, pp. 594–597).

Thomas, Gary S., "Use of Student Notes and Lecture Summaries as Study Guides for Recall" (*Journal of Educational Research,* July–August, 1978, pp. 316–319).

Weiland, Andrea and Kingsbury, Steven J., "Immediate and Delayed Recall of Lecture Material as a Function of Note Taking" (*Journal of Educational Research,* March–April, 1979, pp. 228–230).